SU[...] &ANALYSIS

OF

THE RIGHT SIDE OF HISTORY

How Reason and Moral Purpose
Made the West Great

A GUIDE TO THE BOOK
BY BEN SHAPIRO

TABLE OF CONTENTS

SYNOPSIS

Ben Shapiro's *The Right Side of History: How Reason and Moral Purpose Made the West Great* is a thought-provoking book that dives deep into the historical elements that have made America what it is today. In the book, Shapiro claims that America has abandoned its Judeo-Christian values, which is why the nation is plagued by so much turmoil. The book is an attempt to discuss what the major problems are and how America's soul can be restored.

The book contains nine chapters. Shapiro begins by discussing how true happiness can only be found in embracing Divine law and Godly values. He goes on to show how Judeo-Christian values and Greek reason have been at the forefront of building Western civilization. He gives clear examples of nation-states that abandoned these two ideas and ended up suffering unimaginable atrocities, for example, France during the Revolution, Nazi Germany, and the former USSR. He credits the decline of morality to American Leftists who are intent on creating a society where science is worshiped instead of God. His main premise is that without Divine laws and reason to guide society, America will self-destruct.

Ultimately, the only way to save the country is to revert back to the Judeo-Christian values that once formed the foundation of this great nation. Shapiro states that we must teach our children how to stand up for the truth, no matter the risks involved.

CHAPTER ONE: THE PURSUIT OF HAPPINESS

Shapiro opens the book by trying to explain what happiness is and how politics is merely a framework for the pursuit, not the achievement, of happiness. He identifies the four elements that create happiness in an individual's life as well as society in general. According to him, when any of these ingredients are lacking, happiness becomes impossible to achieve.

Key Takeaway: The Founding Fathers never believed that government could provide happiness.

As a political commentator, Shapiro recognizes the fact that politics isn't the source of his happiness. Politics is merely a way to establish the conditions that usher in happiness in society. Even the Founding Fathers understood that it isn't the role of government to make people happy. The government is only supposed to safeguard your rights and freedoms so that you can get on with the business of pursuing your own happiness. This is something that many Americans have forgotten. It is why Americans are spending more time politicking and fighting political opponents. People mistakenly believe that if the political landscape changes, their lives will be better. It is foolishness to put our faith in politicians.

Key Takeaway: Happiness is only achieved by developing a moral purpose.

More than ever before, America is reeling under the weight of pessimism, fear of the future, and even skyrocketing suicide rates. Shapiro believes that society has stopped pursuing happiness, and instead, people are chasing after money and temporary physical and emotional pleasures. To achieve happiness, you must cultivate your mind and soul and live according to a moral purpose. You must act according to God's will instead of seeking idols such as binge-watching TV shows. Even Aristotle believed in the concept of "*Eudaimonia*," where you act with right reason and live with a virtuous purpose. There is no happiness without virtue, and only those who have a strong sense of purpose can enjoy a long and meaningful life.

Key Takeaway: There are four key elements necessary to develop a moral purpose.

According to Shapiro, generating a moral purpose is the only way to create a proper foundation for happiness. There are four elements that are needed to do this:

Individual Moral Purpose – We are all made in God's image, and everyone must find their God-given mission in life. Part of that mission is to seek God and develop relationships with other people. Without individual moral purpose, people become hedonistic and oppressive toward others, seeking entertaining but useless distractions.

Individual Capacity– Knowing your moral purpose is one thing. Seeking it is something else entirely. If you want to be happy, you must take action to pursue the things that make you happy. You must believe in your ability to make your life better by developing a skillset. You must know who you are and embrace your responsibility to be a productive member of society.

Communal Moral Purpose – Society is made up of groups, which is why individuals feel the need to associate with others. Strong social relationships help you live a longer and happier life. Therefore, to become a proper functioning individual, you need social connections. A community must have a shared vision in terms of its moral purpose. Judeo-Christian values provide a platform on which sound communal values are shared, and without such social ties, a country cannot survive.

Communal Capacity – To pursue a moral purpose as a community, there must be strong social institutions such as social clubs, churches, and charity organizations. Government is also necessary to protect the freedoms of the citizens. However, there must be a balance between government and social organizations. Putting too much emphasis on government as the solution to all our problems only leads to tyranny.

CHAPTER TWO: FROM THE MOUNTAINTOP

Shapiro looks at how Judaism gave mankind meaning, purpose, and birthed Western values. Belief in the Judeo-Christian God is the bedrock of Western civilization and its prosperity. God expects humanity to seek Him and follow His standards of behavior and truth, even though He has granted mankind free will. Forsaking Godly values will be the downfall of Western civilization as we know it.

Key Takeaway: Judaism goes against all the central principles of polytheism.

Thanks to the prevailing Judeo-Christian values, most people today cannot fathom the worship of multiple gods. Yet polytheism used to be the part of many ancient civilizations such as the Romans, Greeks, and Egyptians. According to Shapiro, these pagan or polytheistic cultures believed in a chaotic universe where different gods fought for supremacy. Pagans also believed that God could be physically perceived in natural phenomena, as witnessed today in Eastern religions. However, Judaism is founded on a different set of beliefs.

Judaism claims that there is only one true God who has established specific rules that run the universe. Humans may not always understand God's actions, but according to Judaism, God is moral and just and can never do any wrong. Judaism is not a materialistic faith, and therefore, it is not necessary for us to perceive God with our eyes. The important thing is to believe that He is always with us.

Key Takeaway: Without the Bible, we wouldn't have a standard of moral behavior.

Shapiro argues that prior to the Bible being introduced to mankind, human beings didn't subscribe to a singular code of moral behavior. But with God's commandments, a person would be punished for their sins so that they could learn a moral lesson. God doesn't want us to not be bad; He wants us to be good in the same way that He is good. The pagan sacrifices of the Old Testament were meant to remind people that it's important to change their character rather than merely appease God.

Key Takeaway: Without God, there can be no progress.

The Greeks believed that history was circular and kept repeating itself. The Babylonians believed that the past, present, and future were all connected. The Native Americans, Indians, and Buddhists all believe that time has no beginning or end. But Shapiro contends that history is indeed bound by time. These ancient cultures with their multiple gods were irrational and thus couldn't progress.

According to the Bible, God created man to progress toward his destiny, which is why He chose Israel and led them out of slavery. God wanted to use Israel as a model for the rest of humanity. Even though the Israelites kept sinning, God wants people to learn from their mistakes and ultimately move toward a certain destination—toward Him. God is invested in individuals, and as such, human history cannot be a cyclic loop that has no reason, purpose, or end.

CHAPTER THREE: FROM THE DUST

It's one thing to have faith in God and believe that we are able to choose between right and wrong. That is what Jerusalem gave humanity. However, it's a totally different thing to develop the ability to reason and use logic to overcome human limitations. This is what Greek culture and philosophy gave mankind.

Shapiro argues that in American universities today, radical liberal leftists are trying to destroy the study of the classics. Many professors and students perceive Western civilization to be the root of racism and imperialism, and as such, they are calling for the ban of the study of Greco-Roman philosophies. However, these leftists forget the fact that Western civilization, which has done a lot of good throughout history, is founded on the Athenian framework. Without Greek traditions, the West would not have science, natural law, or even its much-cherished democracy.

Key Takeaway: The role of every individual is to use reason to uncover their purpose.

Most modern philosophers would argue that humans are made up of atoms, life is brutish, and nature has no role to play in our existence. However, Shapiro contends that nature runs according to set rules, and it is our responsibility as humans to decipher those rules to extract our end goals. According to Aristotle and Plato, humans were put on this Earth to judge, reason, and deliberate. By using reason, an individual can find their purpose in life, which is to do the job God created you to do and develop your character along the way. This is how you end up living a virtuous life. In this sense, virtue has less to do with morality and more to do with fulfilling your calling.

Key Takeaway: Science was born out of a need to discover a higher purpose.

To fulfill your calling, you must first identify it; and to find your virtue, you must study nature. The Greeks believed that in order to investigate your purpose, you had to study the rules and systems that govern nature and the universe. For example, Pythagoras discovered mathematics as he was trying to uncover the harmony between humanity and the universe. Plato and Aristotle created the deduction method during their attempt to explain how to find objective truth. In their attempts to understand the physical world around them, the Greeks stumbled upon what we now consider to be the basis of all scientific thinking.

Key Takeaway: America was founded on Cicero's belief in shared governmental responsibility.

Shapiro states that America's democratic roots are based on the Greek ethical government system. The Greeks believed that the city-state is central to human life and a necessary element in an individual's pursuit of virtue. For example, Plato believed that justice is a communal virtue that can only be achieved if the city-state (polis) is run by the wisest philosophers around. The workers should work and the warriors should focus on defending the state. However, Aristotle saw this hierarchical system as a form of totalitarianism and class rule. For there to be checks and balances, the government had to be a hybrid between a democracy and an aristocracy. The American Founding Fathers ultimately preferred Cicero's mixed system where the citizens had some control of the government, with a monarch and the aristocracy all checking each other's powers.

CHAPTER FOUR: COMING TOGETHER

Shapiro describes the conflict between Judaism and Greek thought, and how these two traditions came together to create a modern society founded on both religion and reason.

Key Takeaway: Jewish and Greek cultures were conflicted over three elements.

According to Shapiro, Jewish and Greek thought clashed over three things:

The nature of God – In Judaism, God is always active in the affairs of humans. The Greeks believed that God was not actively involved in human events and thus everything happened as a result of fate.

Universality – The Greeks believed that as long as humans continued to contemplate the world around them, they would eventually become knowledgeable enough to understand all things. The Jews, however, believed that humans were not able to understand all the mysteries of the world and only God's revelation could guide men to the truth.

Individualism – The Greeks believed that individuals should do their best to cultivate virtues that would make them good citizens of the polis. In Judaism, an individual's priority was to be committed to Divine law.

Key Takeaway: Christianity is a combination of Jewish and Greek thought.

The Christian religion borrowed the Jewish vision of God and man's destiny but co-opted the Greek belief in universality. This new religion took the message of Judaism and made it accessible to everyone who chose to put their faith in Christ the Messiah. As a result, it was no longer necessary to abide by Jewish law. Through the grace of God, Jews and Gentiles were now considered equal in the eyes of the Lord.

At the same time, Christianity shattered the Greek belief in reason. With the Gospel of Christ now available to all, there was no need to research and gain knowledge about the world. Humanity could now focus on spiritual undertakings that guaranteed a ticket to heaven.

Key Takeaway: The spread of Christianity across Europe was no accident.

It is estimated that between the year 40 CE and 300, the number of Christians grew from 100,000 to 6 million. There are two possible reasons for this:

1. Christians were known for their love of the poor as well as needy strangers. This commitment to helping the impoverished was a powerful outreach technique.

2. Christianity was the only religion in Europe that was actively engaged in recruiting converts. The fact that it

proposed universal salvation, as well as individual salvation, made it attractive to members of Roman society. Nobody wanted to risk losing out on eternity.

Consequently, while some Roman emperors viewed the new religion as a political threat, others saw it as a way of boosting their power. After Emperor Diocletian's vicious assault on Christianity ended, every successive emperor took a softer stance on the religion until it was finally adopted as the official state religion of Rome in 380 CE.

CHAPTER FIVE: ENDOWED BY THEIR CREATORS

In this chapter, Shapiro expounds on the concept of individual freedom and the natural rights that every human being has. In politics, the Left and the Right often demonize each other in an attempt to force their opinion on the other side. This attempt to create a somewhat one-party state goes against the foundations of eastern civilization. As proven by the conflicts of the past, sharing a common vision does not mean everyone has to pursue the same path toward that vision.

Key Takeaway: Contrary to popular thinking, it is Christians who laid the foundation for scientific advancement.

Many people have been duped into believing that the Church is anti-science and has historically tried to hold back mankind's scientific advancement. This is untrue and historical fact shows otherwise. Shapiro claims that technological advancements became mainstream thanks to Thomas Aquinas, a Christian, and William of Ockham, a Franciscan friar. They used science to prove the need for God and as a way to understand the cosmos. It was the bishop of Lisieux, Nicole Oresme, who discovered that the Earth rotates around its axis. It was the cardinal of Brixen, Nicholas Cusa, who developed the theory that the Earth moves through space and is not stationary. Nicolaus Copernicus, a medical adviser in the church of Warmia, theorized that the Earth rotated around the sun. Even

Galileo, a Christian by faith, believed that science was a way to connect to God.

Key Takeaway: The concept of human rights developed out of a need for religious toleration.

The Thirty Years' War was a religious conflict that led to the death of millions of people in Europe. At the time, the Catholic Church had such massive powers that it was a government unto itself. This centralized authority led some to fight against the papal theocracy. Marsilius believed that people should be allowed the freedom to worship God. Machiavelli disputed the idea that a state can make people virtuous, and as a result, his book, *Prince,* was banned by the Catholic Church in 1559. Men like Luther and Calvin proclaimed that all Christians are equal before God, and thus the priests and bishops are not special or more spiritual. All this led to calls for the devolution of authority away from the pope to the individual.

Key Takeaway: The first individual right was the right to self-preservation.

The political philosopher, Thomas Hobbes, disputed Aristotle's claim that reason was the chief motivator of all humans. As a follower of Machiavelli, Hobbes believed that an individual's primary motivation in life was to save their own skin. This is how all animals operate in nature. When faced with the need for self-preservation, people stop caring about social hierarchies and do all they can to survive. But to prevent a destructive free-for-all, individuals choose to set up a government to ensure that people don't trample on each other's natural rights. These fundamental rights include the right to property, the right to life, and the right to liberty. In the event that the government itself violated the people's natural rights, then the people had a right to rebel and create a new government.

Key Takeaway: The Declaration of Independence is based on Greco-Roman philosophies as well as the Bible.

Shapiro states that the Founding Fathers were students of Cicero, Aristotle, Locke, and the Bible. They based the Declaration of Independence on reason and religion; individual rights and duties; a government with checks and balances; and the pursuit of virtue, both by individuals and society as a whole. All these philosophies are part of natural law, and the Founding Fathers were firm believers in God and the Laws of Nature. It was this belief that led them to proclaim that all men are created equal and are endowed by God with unalienable rights, including life, liberty, and the pursuit of happiness.

CHAPTER SIX: KILLING PURPOSE, KILLING CAPACITY

Key Takeaway: Supporters of Enlightenment view religion as a hindrance to human development.

America is undergoing a conflict that threatens its moral and religious foundation. This conflict revolves around whether the USA is built on secular or religious grounds, with some arguing that curbing religion will make the nation better. Advocates of Enlightenment say that individual rights can only be preserved if religion is abolished and the people embrace reason and materialism. They see God as a barrier that prevents humanity from advancing to greater heights. They also argue that humans don't really have a specific purpose for being.

Shapiro counters this argument by stating that Western civilization is built on both the secular and religious. In fact, Enlightenment borrows heavily from Judeo-Christian values and the Greek concept of purpose. Individual rights and virtue are tenets that are found in the Bible. As history shows, those who have tried to destroy the Judeo-Christian and Greek foundations of the West are responsible for the existential crisis we have today. Reason and disdain for God cannot be used as an excuse to tear down America's foundation.

Key Takeaway: There are three forces that influenced the anti-religion faction.

According to Shapiro, Western civilization shifted from virtue to moral relativism for three reasons:

The end of Catholic dominance – As the influence of Catholicism diminished, religious divisions occurred everywhere, often leading to brutal religious violence. Those opposed to the Judeo-Christian faith saw the religious intolerance as proof that religion is indeed a barrier to human freedom.

Rise of religious fundamentalism – Luther and Calvin saw the Catholic Church as becoming increasingly secular. This forced the Church to deviate from its historical appreciation of secular/scientific learning, thus causing many intellectuals to turn to agnosticism and atheism.

The Peace of Westphalia – As the Catholic Church began to lose control, new minority religions were allowed to grow thanks to the Peace of Westphalia.

Key Takeaway: Moral relativism states that there is no such thing as right or wrong.

Historical characters like Machiavelli, Hobbes, and Spinoza dismissed religion and its moral system as irrational. Machiavelli believed that virtue was not necessary and that a little evil was required to achieve certain outcomes. Hobbes went further by stating that there is no such thing as just and unjust; right or wrong. The only thing that humans care about is achieving power to avoid suffering. Spinoza cast aspersions on the Bible as the word of God, claiming that it was a book that was written for and propagated by foolish people. Moral relativists believe that there is no God or natural law, and as a result, people are free to act however they wish. There is no purpose for being alive, and nobody should foist their moral opinion on others.

Key Takeaway: Without God, morality and purpose can only be found in hedonism.

Once you eliminate God as the source of morality and human purpose, you have to replace Him with something else. And to those who espouse Enlightenment, purpose and morality are found in the pursuit of passion and material things. Darwinism came along to further reinforce the notion that humans were simply a bunch of self-interested animals. But Shapiro argues that those who choose virtue-less reason over God end up creating a world where life is all about enjoying pleasure and minimizing pain. Unfortunately, they soon come to realize that without virtue, humanity easily descends into chaos and tyranny.

CHAPTER SEVEN: THE REMAKING OF THE WORLD

Key Takeaway: The American form of Enlightenment was very different from the French version.

Shapiro contends that two strains of Enlightenment emerged in the Eighteenth century. The American Enlightenment was based on the values espoused by Athens and Jerusalem while the French Enlightenment rejected everything to do with Judeo-Christian values and discoverable purpose. History shows that the American Revolution produced a better outcome because America stuck to its core principles of individual God-given rights, social virtue, and a state that is expected to safeguard these rights.

But the French Revolution was a bloody and violent affair because the French replaced God with moral relativism. Mobs ruled the streets and the priests and kings were executed by guillotine. The Cult of Reason was formed as France's official religion, with *Le Peuple* replacing God. Liberty, equality, and fraternity became the people's rallying cry. Yet by getting rid of Divine and Natural law, the French ended up ceding their individual rights to the nation-state; a situation that would eventually lead to tyranny, nationalism, and a caste system.

Key Takeaway: The French Revolution gave rise to military nationalism as the world had never seen.

After the revolution, France became the first country to force its citizens to join the military. The citizens were subjects of the nation-state and owed their rights to it. Therefore, when France declared war on Austria in 1793, everyone was drafted into the military without exception. Young men would fight, women would make clothes and tents, married men would forge arms, children would convert lint into linen, and the elderly would passionately motivate the soldiers. The Prussian general expected to fight a weak French army but was instead faced with a massive force that defied military odds. It was the first time that the world was witnessing how a government can whip up passions and weaponize its entire population. It was a utopia of nationalism.

Key Takeaway: Social leveling is a utopian ideal that ultimately leads to communism.

One of the motivations of the French Revolution was the need to eliminate class distinctions and instead establish a society where everyone was equal. Aristocrats were viewed as oppressors feeding off of the poor, and property ownership quickly became a crime. Some argued that all private property belongs to society as a whole and must be redistributed to the masses. Capitalism was perceived to be demeaning to humans, and in order to create a new human being in a happy society, capitalism and its Judeo-Christian

God had to be eliminated. This was the first step toward communism.

Key Takeaway: Collective redistributionism and nationalism led to the rise of anti-Semitism in Germany.

The American Founding Fathers believed in the philosophy of meaning—that every individual had a purpose. But thanks to the rise of nationalism, redistributionism, and scientific rule, the individual was relegated to a mere tool to be used for the advancement of the state. In other words, the collective general will was prioritized over individual rights. Shapiro argues that without a sense of morality and stripped of their rights, individuals could no longer check the excesses of the state. As a result, anti-Catholic and anti-Semitic sentiment began to gain a foothold in Otto von Bismarck's Germany. Anyone who professed religion was considered to be an enemy of the state. With the adoption of a similar model of bureaucracy in the United States, President Woodrow Wilson went to the extent of praising Bismarck in 1887 for the admirable system he had created in Germany.

In no time, men like Richard Wagner were claiming that the Germanic people had to emancipate themselves from the yoke of Judaism, plastic Jewish music, and annoying Jewish speech characteristics. After Germany's defeat in WWI, the Nazis arose and kept alight the flame of radical nationalism and racial antisemitism. Lenin and Stalin in

Russia and Mao in China also tried to enforce collectivism in their respective countries. This would eventually lead to some of the worst atrocities in modern history.

CHAPTER EIGHT: AFTER THE FIRE

After WWII, the hopes of a Godless, collectivist society faded as the world tried to recover from the death of millions of people. Instead of science being the answer to mankind's problems, it had almost brought humanity to the brink of extinction. However, the meaning-shaped hole still remained in the heart of Western civilization. Now that God was not a factor and the collective had failed, the only thing left was the individual. Thus the philosophy of existentialism was born.

Key Takeaway: Existentialism was supposed to lead human beings to God, but it somehow led them to worship subjectivity.

Existentialism is a product of the Danish philosopher, Soren Kierkegaard. He saw Enlightenment, universalism, and scientism as deficient ideologies because they tried to seek meaning in things that were outside of man. Kierkegaard believed that meaning and truth were subjective and, therefore, could only be found within the individual. According to Shapiro, Kierkegaard thought that passion was more important than reason, and as a result of looking within, an individual would passionately seek the truth and ultimately find God.

As it turned out, this belief system led to the worship of subjectivity instead. There was no moral truth because all truth was subject to interpretation. The human will was pushed forth as the pinnacle of civilization, and virtues like goodness and honesty didn't matter. Existentialists believe that man is free to do whatever he wants and thus there are no commands from God or natural values that should legitimize his conduct.

Key Takeaway: Throughout history, science has morphed numerous times to become the source of morality.

During the era of Enlightenment, science was perceived to be the only way to free mankind from the shackle of religion. Even after the spectacular failure of scientific government during the two World Wars, people like JFK still believed that science could solve all of mankind's problems. Shapiro states that science continued to morph over time from a way to improve man's material state to something that could enhance the moral condition. But without God or a collective conscience, science then became the source of all morality. The existentialists claimed that science should be the only source of objective truth.

Soon enough, men like Sigmund Freud were claiming that humans were by nature irrational beings that were governed by unknown forces. In other words, there was no reasoning, and if something felt natural, then you should go ahead and do it. You should simply be yourself and accept all your sexual proclivities without judgment.

Key Takeaway: Those who support neo-Enlightenment fail to realize that their cherished values are actually Biblical in nature.

Those who support a neo-Enlightenment claim that Enlightenment simply sprang up into existence and is based solely on reason. Shapiro disagrees and states that the same ideas that neo-Enlightenment advocates believe in are the same as those that form the foundation of Judeo-Christianity and Greek thought. For example, neo-Enlightenment philosophers say that slavery was the result of religion, yet they forget that almost everyone in the abolitionist movement was a Christian. Even Diderot, the self-declared French atheist stated that slavery was a violation of all religious morals. When women were fighting for the right to vote, it was Christian values, not science, which ultimately won them universal suffrage. The Bible clearly states the rights of the individual because we are all made in the image of the Creator. This shows that the concepts of individual liberty and natural rights espoused by neo-Enlightenment advocates weren't an accident. They sprang up from Biblical values.

CHAPTER NINE: THE RETURN TO PAGANISM

In this chapter, Shapiro explains how modern America has forsaken reason and adopted subjectivity as the standard of truth. A man who becomes a transgender woman feels offended when they are referred to as male. As a result, many people now equate reason with intolerance because it suggests that one individual may be more accurate than another. Therefore, the solution is to tear down any kind of moral belief system and instead return to the ancient customs of animalistic passion and paganism that preceded societal norms.

Key Takeaway: The Left has always tried to paint America as a cultureless and intolerant nation.

From the 1940s to the 1960s, America was a nation where religion was a pillar of strength. Despite sexism and racism, women were increasingly being allowed into the workforce and more black people were joining high-level occupations. America was also steeped in culture, with millions of people watching orchestras, reading historical books, and watching cultural programs on TV. Yet all the American Left saw was a capitalistic country that was intolerant to minorities and foreign cultures. This led to the belief that the only way to bring about freedom for all people was to tear down the system.

Key Takeaway: The clash between capitalism and Marxism is predicated on a false narrative.

According to Shapiro, Marxists believe that American materialism will ultimately lead to totalitarianism and fascism. Marxists view capitalism as a way of enslaving humans and creating automatons that cannot think for themselves; a nation with people who are sexually repressed and victimized. This kind of thinking is what led to the sexual revolution and counterculture movement that swept the media and academia in the 60s and 70s.

Proponents of Marxism equate capitalism to Nazism, but the truth is that Marxism has more in common with Nazism than capitalism ever will. While it may be true that capitalism has created a materialistic culture and many other societal ills, the solution does not lie in destroying the system. The answer is to restore the founding American system of values.

Key Takeaway: Telling kids that they are special has created a self-obsessed generation.

Abraham Maslow believed that the ultimate goal of every human being was self-realization. However, this concept was hijacked by the New Left as a way to steer the masses toward self-fulfillment. Repression is an obstacle to realizing our deepest desires, and since repression starts in childhood, the parenting style had to change. In 1946, Dr. Benjamin Spock began preaching the theory that in order to raise kids who have healthy self-esteem, parents had to remove restrictions on their children. Soon enough, poor self-esteem was blamed for all the ills in society. As a result, instead of disciplining or criticizing kids for bad behavior, parents started to let them follow their own will. Self-esteem was thus elevated as the most important path to true self-realization and success in life.

Shapiro claims that instead of creating a generation of fulfilled people, we now have people who think that everything they do is special. As research would later show, self-esteem doesn't make you a high achiever—your achievements are what elevate your self-esteem. But today we have cartoon characters and celebrity singers telling the youth that everyone is special and there is no right or wrong way to behave.

Key Takeaway: Free speech is under attack thanks to intersectionality.

Intersectionality is a state of belonging to more than one minority group. Since minorities have traditionally been marginalized, it has created a situation where the voice of minorities is supposed to carry more weight than those who are considered "less victimized." For example, a black female Muslim lesbian is deemed to be more victimized than a white male Christian heterosexual. Therefore, when the former speaks about institutional bigotry in America, the latter should acknowledge that they have benefited from white male privilege. Anyone who does not support the views of intersectional people is thus considered a bigot.

This has led to a situation where freedom no longer applies to everyone in equal measure. Freedom is now a tool that can only be used to protect intersectional people and their need for self-realization. Even when someone uses scientific studies to highlight the inherent differences between races or genders, they are quickly called out as racist or sexist. Shapiro contends that the Left is willing to attack anyone who tries to discuss issues that are likely to debase the self-esteem of intersectional people. Unfortunately, by deliberately denying perceived beneficiaries of the system their freedom of speech, the Left is gradually driving more people to join the alt-right movement.

EDITORIAL REVIEW

In *The Right Side of History*, controversial and conservative writer Ben Shapiro tries to explain why America is hurtling down the path to destruction. The book is a chronological attempt to try to figure out how America lost its foundational values and how it can recover them.

America has always had problems in the past—racism, income inequality, political divisions. But what we are seeing today borders on the unimaginable. Shapiro argues that the same people who have benefitted from Western civilization have forgotten the core values that make it a great nation. The Liberal Left is at the forefront of America's destruction, labeling anyone who opposes their agenda a bigot. He references the mayhem that occurred during his 2015 speaking tour, as protesters tried their best to prevent him from exercising his right to free speech. Shapiro stands firmly by his religious values and believes that abortion and homosexuality are sins.

An interesting aspect of Shapiro's book is the fact that he places a lot of weight on Judeo-Christian values and Greek natural law. He believes that every nation that has rejected these twin ideals has ended up in destruction, for example, the USSR, Venezuela, and Nazi Germany. Therefore, as America continues to abandon its foundational Judeo-Christian values in exchange for scientific law, nationalism, and humanism, it too will self-destruct.

He quotes the Bible often, which is no surprise as he has never been shy of expressing his Jewish roots. He states that happiness can only come by taking the right action according to the will of God. And since Divine meaning and reason are the twin pillars of happiness, it's the Jews and the ancient Greeks who are responsible for providing the ideas necessary for a functioning society. However, he conveniently forgets that other continents and peoples have had their own great cultures throughout history and have contributed to what we today call Western civilization. On top of that, it's a bit of a stretch to say that there is no morality without the Bible. What about cultures that predated Christianity? Didn't they have their own set of values and moral codes?

Shapiro's writing style and tone are academic and formal. He provides a ton of historical research to back up some of his claims. If you are a student of history, you will enjoy the book, but if you aren't, then you may find some parts of the book tedious to read. There are some interesting parts though, especially in Chapter 7 where he describes the French Revolution and its aftermath. Clearly, the author doesn't think very highly of the French and the way they choose to do things.

As the book nears its conclusion, you can see that Shapiro begins to take a swipe at Leftists for their disdain for God and religion. He sees their attempt to replace Divine law with science, all in the name of "change," as a threat to Western civilization. Leftists are pretending to be fighting for Blacks and gays but their true agenda is to replace capitalism with socialism and create a society with no morals.

Ultimately, America's salvation lies in restoring Judeo-Christian values and teaching the next generation how to defend the Divine truth—purpose, possibility, gratitude, and respect for all life.

BACKGROUND ON AUTHOR

Ben Shapiro is an American bestselling author, lawyer, conservative radio show host, political commentator, and podcaster. He has written 10 books including *Brainwashed: How Universities Indoctrinate America's Youth* and *Bullies: How the Left's Culture of Fear and Intimidation Silences Americans*. He wrote his first book at the age of 17 and went on to become America's youngest syndicated columnist.

Born in Los Angeles on January 15, 1984, to Jewish parents, Benjamin Aaron Shapiro attended Walter Reed Middle School before graduating from Yeshiva University High School in 2000. In 2004, he graduated *summa cum laude* with a B.A. in political science from the University of California, Los Angeles. He went on to acquire his JD from Harvard Law School in 2007, before starting his own law firm in 2012.

He went on to work for *Breitbart News* as editor-at-large but resigned in 2016 after falling out with the conservative website. He co-founded *The Daily Wire* in 2015 and is currently its editor-in-chief. He is also a columnist for *Newsweek* and *Creators Syndicate*. He also hosts *The Ben Shapiro Show*, an online political podcast.

Shapiro is an ardent pro-life supporter and vehemently opposes gay marriage. He has been married to Mor Toledano since 2008 and together they have two children.

TITLES BY BEN SHAPIRO

The Right Side of History: How Reason and Moral Purpose Made the West Great (2019)

True Allegiance (2016)

What's Fair and Other Short Stories (2015)

A Moral Universe Torn Apart (2014)

The People vs. Barack Obama: The Criminal Case Against the Obama Administration (2014)

Bullies: How the Left's Culture of Fear and Intimidation Silences America (2013)

Primetime Propaganda: The True Hollywood Story of How the Left Took Over Your TV (2011)

Project President: Bad Hair and Botox on the Road to the White House (2008)

Porn Generation: How Social Liberalism Is Corrupting Our Future (2005)

Brainwashed: How Universities Indoctrinate America's Youth (2004)

END OF BOOK SUMMARY

Made in the USA
Lexington, KY
14 May 2019